Rachel Blum's exquisite book, *The Doctor of Flowers*, is at once a transcendent journey in which the natural world acquires the resplendence of sublime realms and a beautiful and tender elegy for a young daughter. A heartbreaking masterpiece.

—**Steffen Horstmann,** UJJAIN and JALSAGHAR

Rachel Blum's first book of poems, *The Doctor of Flowers*, is nothing less than beautiful and profound. Her work is at once full of pain and the elements of its relief. Blum refuses to look away from pain—indeed she travels with it, taking turns following its lead and leading it to a better end herself. Reading her work involves a deep trust between poet and reader, and it's worth every line of that emotional connection. Her poetic world makes grief into an atmosphere of surprising livability—circulating, moveable, and spirit-filled.

—**Eric Wertheimer,** REGULUS and MYLAR

As the Japanese art of *kintsugi* repairs shattered pottery with gold and platinum, making it more cherishable, *The Doctor of Flowers* enters and runs through our bruised hearts and mends them with immense healing beauty.

—**Eryk Hanut,** THE ROAD TO GUADALUPE and THE RUMI CARDS AND BOOK

The Doctor of Flowers

The Doctor of Flowers

POEMS

Rachel Blum

THREE: A TAOS PRESS

Book Design & Typesetting: Lesley Cox,
FEEL Design Associates, Taos, NM
Press Logo Design: William Watson, Castro Watson,
New York, NY
Front Cover Artwork: *The Starship*, Aron Wiesenfeld,
San Diego, CA
Author Photograph: Joe Chielli, Philadelphia, PA

Text Typeset in Cochin and Axiforma
Printed in the United States of America by
Cottrell Printing Company

ISBN: 978-0-9972011-7-8

THREE: A TAOS PRESS
P. O. Box 370627
Denver, CO 80237
www.3taospress.com

10 9 8 7 6 5 4 3 2 1

For Michaela

In Memory of Isabel
10 November 1990 ~ 14 May 2001

III.

IV.

V.

At night you are carrying
a bouquet of phantom roses,

their fragrance a sensation of
lost parts,

the body still riding
a bareback horse,

the dawn beach
infinite pearls

beneath
galloping.

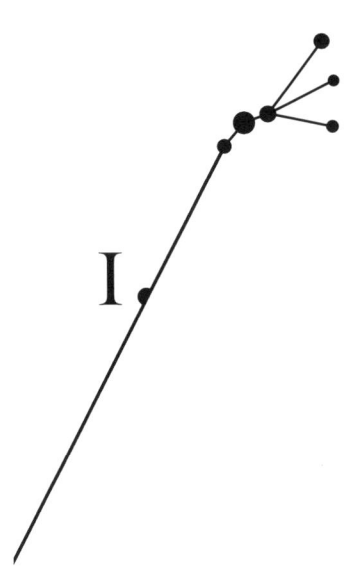

I.

The unfathomable part of death is love.
So we invented the soul to be its ship.

Because what is the soul
if not the collection of our loves.

Distilled to a form like the hull
blooming into dark water.

And as full of meaning
as the soft face of the horses.

I counted days
as if

the sentence from which
to subtract them is measured.

Counted them as if in the end
the measure could alter the light.

As if in the end the measure
would alter darkness.

The night of her diagnosis
I dreamed her white spiral
like a small galaxy
that rose away
from the hospital gurney
and turned back only once.

With a face like the monk's face.
Its jagged stones of a riverbed
with water washing over them
like a love that crosses
the constellations
as a secret planet

to something personal like this loneliness.
Whose magnet is strongest at twilight.
As if an astronaut's life
had been mine and really I
was torn from the ship
and floating among stars
with home a distant blue glass.

Long before illuminated leaves
spill over roads
for the recognition of light,

a child is offered
to a monastery,
to birth her perfect longing,

for the invisible universe
whose faces she sees
in the pattern of stars.

The astronauts
are heartbroken.
Back home autumn
gathers in the yard,

while the ship records
sapphire oceans
and white hieroglyphs
of storms.

It is Jalal ad-Din Muhammad Rumi's birthday.
After months my dreams wake up

in prayer
I think I fathom.

The tears are verses.
My friend is walking out of her body.

Intricate patterns
of loving

breathe on the doors while
the famous and the unrecorded

teachers of peace
answer—

The heart is always this particular child.
The doctor of flowers

is always
counting beyond measure.

—for Seemi Ghazi

If love is always
a rediscovered one,
war too must be
relocated binding,

when we part
the grasses of the earth
that are our mother's hair,
and find a scar of place,

a vulnerable site,
the bell shape
of a grief always
returned to ringing.

In the room
where the soul stops
to rest before traveling,
the beds are full
of children.

And the angels,
kneeling in lab coats,
are working at folding
their wings like flags
for torn families.

In the soul's hospital room,
friends bring flowers,

their petals the shapes of stars
in colors that dignify an old shame.

Violet for the parents
on the sea's horizon line

and white for going mute
while the walls sing a rhythm

of the sickroom ventilator.
And when the doctor comes in

from the night hallway,
the soul stands and folds her soul

into an origami house.
The garden of paper fortunes.

In the same year
time came to our house,
the mapmaker
returned to my dreams,

and if I called him,
it was in a dark language
of animal faces.
Solitary before

bridges made
of the 4 a.m. rain,
or in temporary
pairs while light

fell on hollow trees.
We spoke once, and I
showed you this despair.
Beneath the surface,

fish turned gold
in black water
and swam through
the folds.

I met you
in a dream
and loved
your dreambody,

and saw on it
the light patterns
of flower petals,

visible to bees
and to the faithful
to the god of the river,

winding as
snakewater,
half animal
and the other
half tears.

We are in a night room.
There is a book, and
the passages you loved
are marked in paper colors.

One wall is glass
and beyond it water
in the way of the ocean
reaching the horizon.

A field of reflection
with music that fills the air
with the same infinite quality,
somehow, of full silence.

It is a relief to the soul
when opposites meet like this,
and everyone sees it
without contradiction.

When spirits look out
from their tossed bed sheets
and beyond the window glow,
halos of the morning sun.

There was a place to cry.

I was thirty.

The girls had become babies
in a nine months' dream
where bodies meet
the multicolored
infinity.

Imagining the dream,
it is swords first
and then the empress.
Walking out of Frida Kahlo
or into Georgia's flower.
This double umbilicus
knotted into
the illuminated garden.

They wake to sensuality
and the shock of hunger,
the sky a recognizable gate
to each direction,
and pieces of old lanterns
securing white fields.

Don't go yet. Shadows of the maple and elm have formed one mass on the lawn, after years of standing next to each other. I feel their restraint, the fleeting light, or their interpretation of it. Think of the one who nursed the whole day she was born, or the clematis, that climbs on and blooms in front of the houses.

In the recurring fantasy
where I've stopped
on a busy highway,
cars speeding by,
then slowing
to honk,
until one
quiets to a melody,
having seen
I am resting my head
on the cold steering wheel,
asleep nearly,
as in a hypothermia
and almost dreaming.

That one
taps the glass.
Here now, he says,
like in the movie
where the cop's
as gentle as
the wife is crazy,
when she
needs a rest,
from hills
of sadness,
her blouse
is barely
covering.

Thank you

for your translation
of the night;
it is in my native
language.

And I carried
the bottle of soil
from that lost yard
over every border.

Letters forgotten
like tablets on a wheel.
And the colors
alternating in waves

that arrive on
the sands of
the soul's five
sadnesses.

And the jar is always
full of questions.
And the garden
grows beckoning.

II.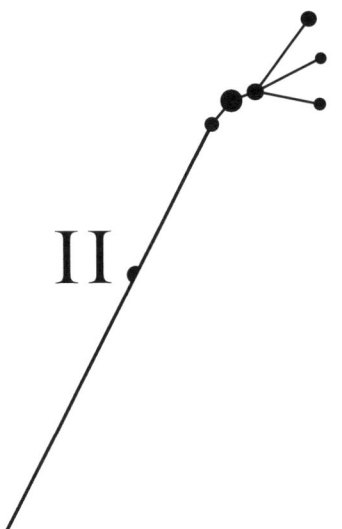

In a dream
where the face
never appears,
the first night doctor
speaks from India,
in a voice without edges,
and on a cot nearby
a nurse stays the night,
and draws a bed curtain
around the darkness.

In gentlest hands,
with ancient windows
for open palms,
your innocence
is cradled,
in rooms where
time is growing.

And in the middle
of the building,
near a moss covered
onyx fountain,
a lamb is being born,
the father pacing
rings around her.

Carry bells
through dreams
up hills
to fields
where sun
falls in
puddles, light
like steep
climbs toward
doves drawn
permanently
over hearts

turning toward
moons falling
like rain,
light like
a horse-drawn
ceremony
at last —

What could you be thinking
sweet ember —

worry crossing
your face now
like the shadow
of a wren.

I am asked to select one memory. You and I are
in the infusion center at Children's Hospital of
Philadelphia. You are making a rubber band ball
while you receive chemotherapy. The nurses swim
out into the water through a window in the wall.
They seem to come and go this way from the sea.
One night in New Mexico, you woke me to say
that your head was hurting. The day before you
had confused a camera and a telephone; I'd been
photographing crosses, but when we got back
to the hotel, you spoke into my camera. Later, in
the Albuquerque emergency room, you felt better
and read a book. A doctor led me into a small
dark room full of other doctors. They asked me
about the pictures of your brain and offered me
a telephone calling card. By gardens outside
of the hospital, I sat on the sidewalk and cried.
Once your diagnosis was confirmed, I cried only
privately, as if I had no clothing. Flying home,
the four of us saw a rainbow from the airplane.
You leaned on my arm and slept. Every week in
the oncology clinic we sat next to each other like
two people on a train, cozy and set apart from the
world. In the panic and grace of those afternoons,
it was as if we would last—your soul had turned
down this road, and I would be with you. And it
was as if we'd died—our bodies already thinned to
light, and still I was with you. When your surgeon
said to me, *This is the most difficult thing you will
ever do*, I borrowed his loose uniform, wrapped
like a priest's collar, bloody from battle, or hanging
clean on a sun-drenched southern clothesline.
I remember you best with my hands. In my hands,
it is always the same day.

—for John

Maybe this is as far as the conversation goes.
You tell me a story and I draw
the dot-to-dot of loss,
and you say, *Let's stop now*.

I say *Okay*, and you send over
a rainbow box of markers.
I draw a couple
of stars in my palm,
and we hold hands for awhile.
And our hands
are the two shells
at the beginning of this pearl.

In the hospital waiting room,
I ask for the future
and imagine your lab coat
with red letters spelling
a married name,
a specialty

of the hearts of childhood
friends grieving freely.
A tribe crying for
when we knew each other,
and were no older than you.

Here, in the failing body
of an old friend's daughter,
I revisit layers of your face.
A level half immortal,
half suffering
luminosity,

to me,
as the sudden flowers,
or gentle horse souls'
apparent knowing,
she is as you were,
already a cardiologist.

Beyond the window
a tree in coronation,

while you ready for this,
our most imagined voyage —

Here, branches of flowers.
Colors appearing on wood.
Small chartreuse pages
curved without letters,
like the delicate lips
of a baby content with sound.
Meaning already enough
in the wild vowels
that climb the light trellis
like roses.

There, a highway runs
by a frozen lake.
Or if the night
is not austere,
the silver underfeathers
of angels who have
taken you in their arms.
And how one seems
to resemble a friend I lost.

Her Madonna eyes and
white wisps of summer
night parties where flowers
glowed on stems.
A few of them weeping.
Their petals like sails.
And the night air like
waters of a darkening sea.
While across the yard
in a corner near the garage
a figure is painting
the maps on the eggs
with a brush full of stars.

—for Emily Leonard

Soul is
without body,
it is
without thinking,
with love
a rhythm
of ocean,
an intelligent
gravity, or
shine of
garden traced
to render
how it is
I knew you.

In this dream
I am writing
in the shape
of a horse,
her tail
like smoke
or wind,
her breath
frost or
the white
energy of
an angel
whose spirit
she mouths —
she is
not sensible
anymore.

worried doll
storm green sky

unmapped
expanse of forest

the animal voices
unidentified

the compass
too weak

Polaris
too far away

unmoored toddler
lost in crowds

with the Atlantic
a gray monster

small body
in the tub of stars

with porcelain
and lavender

memory
too mortal

a horse
riding feathers

away love
he is too heavy

to carry
the opalescent

spine snapping
weight giving way

In April, the girls drew pictures for the house,
and the local shop didn't charge us for the framing.
Isabel drew the house surrounded by butterflies,
the sun rising in the west. Michaela made a thick-
stemmed flower, with a huge blossom reaching
the clouds. And that same week, two friends drew
identical sky flowers, little girls who had not been
over to visit, but who heard, somehow, a verse
the soil sent that spring.

Like everything else, it is different with children,
a hospital child development specialist told me.
Each morning at breakfast, I listened to the brief
song I loved. Isabel advised me never to eat alone.
Michaela, six years old then, remarked that she'd
been feeling emotional for several days. We sat
outside under the blooming dogwood tree. Another
tree needed to come down, and we saved a bag of
sawdust they gathered from the grass around the
old trunk. I memorized a Latin name and drove
them to school where the fourth graders were
keeping busy, folding a thousand paper cranes.
Until one Friday afternoon, when Isabel said that
she was tired and needed the wheelchair after all.

Calla lily,

your one continuous petal —

a cape for the children,
awake in their beds,
and breathing

unevenly.

III.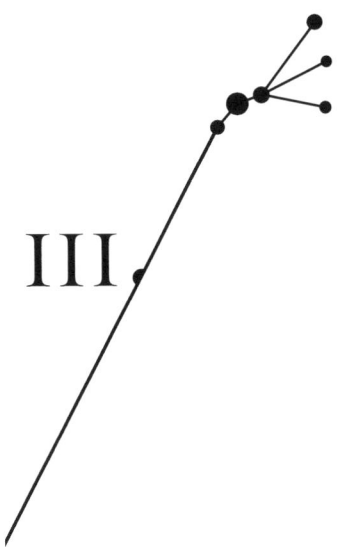

After the funeral
in a quiet corner of the garden
sun lighting young grass
and birds flown from markers,
the dog carrying
the sleek black
river of his body,

a god inside
tells

love everything

in a voice of burning through

an eleventh commandment.

No one is falling
from the sky tonight.

My body a blue arc,
the eggs are white stars

with light years away melodies
someone will compose you.

—for Isabel

Another verse on the stars

on the glass top of rivers

on the dream bicycle

a knit cap for the bell

for the paperboy

for notifying your teachers

that you are coming from
our breakfast kitchen

and the morning candle
that cuts the damp —

can I send it with you?

A mother flows through us. In our dreams,
she appears on a winter night, in a city forest.
For you, she is a couple dressed in black,
in a stained glass building, named for an artist.
In this building, you say, anyone can come,
for free, to pray. This is a return, you say.
Night after night my greenhouse is built.
The first pane, a transparent elevator in
the neurosurgery suite of the hospital. Next,
the old phone booth between the Quaker
meetinghouse and the gymnasium. Eventually,
mosaic children. And a small mountain
cathedral in Colorado, with orange-pink
clouds of a sunset, throughout all hours. Plants
arrive quietly. They are the green colors of May
birdsong, with lilies the glass magnifies.
And not far off, the couple stirs constellations,
giving Sagittarius a violin.

—for Michaela

If the world is infinite
by way of these stories
and their alternatives,

by the mind's capacity
to hear, and the heart's
to sail

toward and against
a discovered wind —
an uncovered other one —

then the stairway imagined
in grief,
or concert in a dream,

where beneath the front lawn sycamore
you sing, mouth sealed
in that way of the dead,

face emanating
in that way of the animals,
this song of the wheels.

I see you were given
larger wings,

changing that small body
I sent morning candles

to light
my imagined darkness.

Taller than I,
you arrive on sorrow's water.

A mark of light
in my peripheral vision,

or tap of loving,
an expanding path.

Walking around
the autumn pond,
I am briefly
inside jewels.

The spirit
sees differently
at the margins
of feeling,

with loss like the moon
on a transparent night,
when the shadow's
a discernible territory,

where they've left the stars on
long past school time.

The archaeologist shifts
the gravel over an old prison

for a silhouette
of the birds on the wall.

A wood chariot
with wheels turning

in the direction of flowers.
For their invention of velvet.

The wisdom masters teach
the unseen world is here.

A half step corridor
of dream residents.

Or the time you thought
you felt Jesus

inhabiting a guy at Starbucks
whose small kindness

could be mistaken
for manners.

But entered the body instead
and expanded beyond it.

Immeasurable heart.
Electric flower.

Somewhere in the future is a flame.
A cup of ash and blue light
or a mirror spark of conception.
Perhaps we precede it as the soul
precedes the idea of a baby.
With a leap of faith
into that small dependent body.
With limbs like fragile stems
and the small fist a closed violet.
And foreknowledge a constellation.
With stars like bones and
petals that cry open and settle
like waves on the familiar sea.
And the larger night blooming
flower of authority
with its shadow on the walls.
And the complicated skull
with its shifting map of plates and hinges
that to the soul might resemble
a traditional prayer.

Years later, and still
the dawn birds
sing Kaddish
in remembrance
and in magnification
and in praise.
A series of notes
that reach through time
from a golden country
just below the heavens.
And the trees too
are blossoming crowns,
are gifts in the doorway,
or blessings for a hidden
bridge home.

—for Isabel

May the golden thread be woven
through your clothing
in all seasons,

the tree of life growing
flowers and food at once,
her shade the grand mother

who already
pulls her love
from heaven.

May the thigh of White Tara
be yours, so every joy
is also holding hands with God.

May her alchemical halo be yours,
so that any loneliness
will find its radiance

and disappear
in Whitman's grasses
and in other friendships.

May the rainbow horse be yours.
When—here—your childhood
returns in scenes

that gallop like hearts
in all of time's directions,
may ancestors bring blessing to you.

— for Michaela

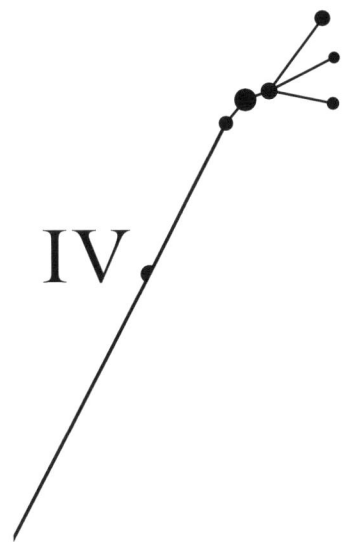

IV

Who will you hold
in the next world
if there is no river
of forgetfulness?

When the body's water
    carries her soul to Lethe,

the ocean will be full of spirits,
    and rain, intended gifts.

There,
    in freed giving,

a meaning
    of healing.

In the market
weeks before her death,

Isabel held out a pomegranate
and remarked on Persephone's

good fortune of reunion.
The myth was a net and pool.

Building
becomes tears.

Caught on the surface
a hair in the shape of a number

asking
why sit so long

by the underground streams,
their liquid black diamonds.

Persephone is eight.
The fish, mercury angels.

In time for a boat,
doves carry the alphabet.

They have known for so long
they already resume their singing—

There is never what is lost—

the years spent
trying to learn this,

the footsteps halting
softly

over the house.

She will recognize
by gold stitching,

Demeter promised
by patterning,

with flowers as vows
beneath a contractual moon

the water enfolds her
in her loves.

Sometimes I see us
at two ends of the same river,

sea bottles arriving
filled with text

or silk plants

or empty

but for a wind note
of shells.

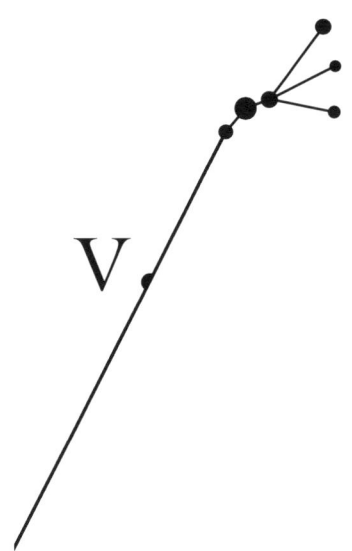

V

It was a season of messengers,
men of barely disguised antiquity
driving modern cars,
pages arriving at night
blank but for names
or filled with song
or a letter from ancestors.
These are visitations—
a horse riding through a veil,
a wall that becomes mist.

Last night I saw you in the kitchen
you were crying you were
never more beautiful
in a play it was called
The Phoenix. The housecoat
is print flowers
and the following days
are marked trails.

—for Jane Lieberman Blum

It is a lullaby.

Hush, my hand is warm on your hair.
The man will return in your dream
carrying a clipboard
bearing one word,
a name of one mind.
A point on a map,
the mind a drawer
full of constellations,
gods that by a different author
might have been flowers.

Hush, the stars
are making no requests
tonight, they are dead
on their light's arrival,
and have no conditions

for singing.

We're a glimpse
of something beautiful,
a distant star,
that candle going out.
Coming back
is the law of the garden
for some of the flowers.

And the rose is named for her,
the one who finds a way.

We remember
an ancient chapter,
sand bell shape
of solitary,
though love
was the law of the garden,
the winding of river.

And the rose is named for her,
the one who finds a way.

In the girls' Oz,
we are flying over mountains.
On a porch made of driftwood,
Dorothy rocks, elderly now.
Her hair is polished silver,
her friends are long infinite,
their missing pieces
years returned to them.

Outside, the world
is saturated with a light
that is audible
just out of range,
the twin sister
of the shell's dark
and faraway earth song,
born in smooth pink
like a human baby.

Over the loudspeaker
voices braid together
to form a pilot.
We are not landing.

When the ship enters deep space
and ocean becomes memory,
among silent glass colors
of the forward constellations —

Where is this underworld?
If it is not the final box
of a keeper of the hearth
who let the light go out,
or the parallel grasses
of a long and faithful waiting,
for visitors like trains.

I am sure the body translates
a language opaque as stars.
Sometimes we slow to its cadence
and love with a sensation
that must be what the trees know,
I am sure fire knows.

The long distance healers have
a point about collecting prayers.
This is our ocean.
Hope inhabits it —
a school of golden fish
in an underwater
column of sunlight.

Imagine gathering all
of the aesthetic talent
over miles and years,
or all first day love,
or the entire machine of flowers.
Grief joins each other.
This is our broken tree,
our birds flying regardless,
musical and iridescent.

In a low voice

will be

a tone of violets

in fields
prior razed.
Stems glow
with the morning light,
as do trophies,
and city hospitals,
the passengers
of a fleet
of imaginary ships,
minds resting
on gurneys

cording stars,

the polished hospital floor

a vase of nurses.

In temple
between my daughters,
one passed
ten years now,
so one in form
and one a cloud
of light still
reaching for my hand,
a concentration in the air,
or sound from a shell
ground to sand
a thousand years ago —
while the other
takes my hand
in hers, as if
she feels her
sister near
as when
they lay
against each other,
kittens in a box
of sunlight or
cord connected
birds —

two parts
of the one body —
mine —
soul hopes —
one here
and one there,
and all among us
this random
crossing over
to violet.

— On Rosh Hashanah

This moment of giving voice to a blossom.
Vibrating with its singularity in the immeasurable
universe. One open bud, with her velvet curtains.
One white star, distant, hot and frozen, always
indicating. The newest baby in the family, wet
from another world. Or in the soul's hospital, one
of the ones, bidding goodbye to the loves of this
lifetime. The flower seems not to mind when we
rest from the truth; it is as happy to be our comfort
as our object of study. Unfolded and open beneath
the microscope. Energetic in the colors of so many
different kinds of welcoming. Or still and quiet,
in the vase by the hospice bed, resonating with
wilting. We do not know whether there is any pain
associated with it. The unforgettable last breath
comes and we can no longer ask. Imagination
takes over and the beloved walks into us.

At the universal gem
I travel your holiness,

your invisible love,
a silent palpable music.

All of our lost ones
return in undefined tears,

their heads bowed
in uncategorized longing,

while we mirror
our longing for them.

Between wakefulness
and sleep

are repeating visions—
small groups of figures.

I look for you,
among the similarly aged—

but they are wind
and hair and sunlight,

and only the gleaming
is named.

—On Yom Kippur

Who would have come
if the angel had not come

*Was there something
you wanted to tell me*

A river flowed
through my house

*so there is nothing
you cannot say to me*

Water that
begins in the stairs
carries a velvet dress

like plaster
when my legs
are failing

and salt like snow
so suddenly
your laughter

and the sound
is a boat and the
boat is my hands

and I remember you best
with my hands

there it is always
the same day

I would like to thank the dream taxi drivers
For the impossible journey over water
And the undetermined flat rate
From Canada to Maryland
From a family name
To an undisclosed
Desert location.

In lieu of flowers
Is the river
Conceived on the back steps
Of a loneliness
That became a song
Who in form
Would be a wing
The light
That is a hand.

Thank you to Andrea Watson and 3: A Taos Press for the recognition, encouragement, guidance, and support, without which this book would not have been possible.

Thank you to Michael Sells for reading my poems with nurturing generosity over many years.

The encouragement and support of my online community of friends, writers, and artists were indispensable in the making of this book. Thank you to everyone who read and appreciated my poems, for the gift of growing confidence.

For reading the manuscript and offering kind words, many thanks to Doug Anderson, Eryk Hanut, Steffen Horstmann, Michael Sells, and Eric Wertheimer.

For his beautiful painting, *The Starship*, many thanks to Aron Wiesenfeld.

For sensitive and masterful design, many thanks to Lesley Cox.

Gratefulness and love to my family for standing by me and for supporting the sharing of experience in writing.

To Michaela and Isabel, my gratefulness exceeds anything that I could write. But it is my hope that these words will be to your spirits a love and strengthening, as your being is to mine.

Grateful appreciation is made to the editors of the following publications in which these poems first appeared, sometimes in different versions:

American Literary Review: "It was a season of messengers…," "It is a lullaby…," "In the girls' Oz…"

California Quarterly: "In the same year…," "We are in a night room…," "I see you were given…," "The archaeologist shifts…," "The long distance healers have…"

Confrontation: "Don't go yet…"

Journal of Feminist Studies in Religion: "In this dream…," "In temple…"

Live Encounters Poetry: "If love is always…," "In the room…," "I met you…," "Thank you…"

Mayo Review: "It is Jalal ad-Din Muhammad Rumi's Birthday…"

Saint Katherine Review: "Long before illuminated leaves…," "In the soul's hospital room…," "At the universal gem…"

Shambhala Times: "The unfathomable part of death is love…"

Taos International Journal of Poetry and Art: "After the funeral…," "Who would have come…"

Vox Populi: "The night of her diagnosis…"

Rachel Blum graduated from Haverford College with a BA in English Literature and Creative Writing. She studied writing at New York University under Galway Kinnell, Sharon Olds, and Yehuda Amichai. Her poems have appeared in literary journals including *American Literary Review*, *Journal of Feminist Studies in Religion*, and *Taos Journal of International Poetry and Art*. She has taught creative writing to patients at Goldwater Hospital in New York City, at PATH Community Mental Health Center in Philadelphia, and to children at the Philadelphia Center for Grieving Children, Teens, and Families. She is a longtime reiki practitioner, working in private practice and as a volunteer at Children's Hospital of Philadelphia, after many years serving as a volunteer in the reiki program of the Abramson Cancer Center of the Hospital of the University of Pennsylvania.

I was nine years old the winter of church. Entering hymns like summer ferns, light caught the forest floor, unveiling these waters of the air. The choir wove swaddling from voices. The first god was sensation, a music preceding believing. My father's family are German Jews, my mother's German Mennonites. Family is a river too, taking turns where mountains rise from matter and finally the oceans collect us. A church happened by music. Sanctuary happened when the notes of the universe bowed their heads in meditation, together composing an awesome silence.

Aron Wiesenfeld's artwork has been the subject of eight solo exhibitions in the United States and Europe since 2006. Among the publications in which his work has appeared are *Juxtapoz, Hi-Fructose, Art In America,* and *The Huffington Post.* His work has been in a number of museum shows, including The Long Beach Museum of Art, Bakersfield Museum of Art, and The Museum Casa Dell'Architettura in Italy. His paintings have been used for covers on nine books of poetry, including *The Other Sky,* a collaborative book project with poet Bruce Bond. In 2014, a large monograph of his work titled *The Well* was published by IDW Press.

Collecting Life: Poets on Objects Known and Imagined – Madelyn Garner and Andrea Watson

Seven – Sheryl Luna

The Luminosity – Bonnie Rose Marcus

Trembling in the Bones: A Commemorative Edition – Eleanor Swanson

3 A.M. – Phyllis Hotch

Ears of Corn: Listen – Max Early

Elemental – Bill Brown

Rootwork – Veronica Golos

Farolito – Karen S. Córdova

Godwit – Eva Hooker

The Ledgerbook – William S. Barnes

The Mistress – Catherine Strisik

Library of Small Happiness – Leslie Ullman

Day of Clean Brightness – Jane Lin

Bloodline – Radha Marcum

Hum of Our Blood – Madelyn Garner

Dark Ladies & Other Avatars – Joan Roberta Ryan